"For fast-acting relief, try slowin
-Lily Tomlin

www.TranscendenceShop.com

"Sometimes the most important thing in a whole day is the rest we take between two deep breaths."
-Etty Hillesum

"How beautiful it is to do nothing, and then to rest afterward." -Spanish Proverb

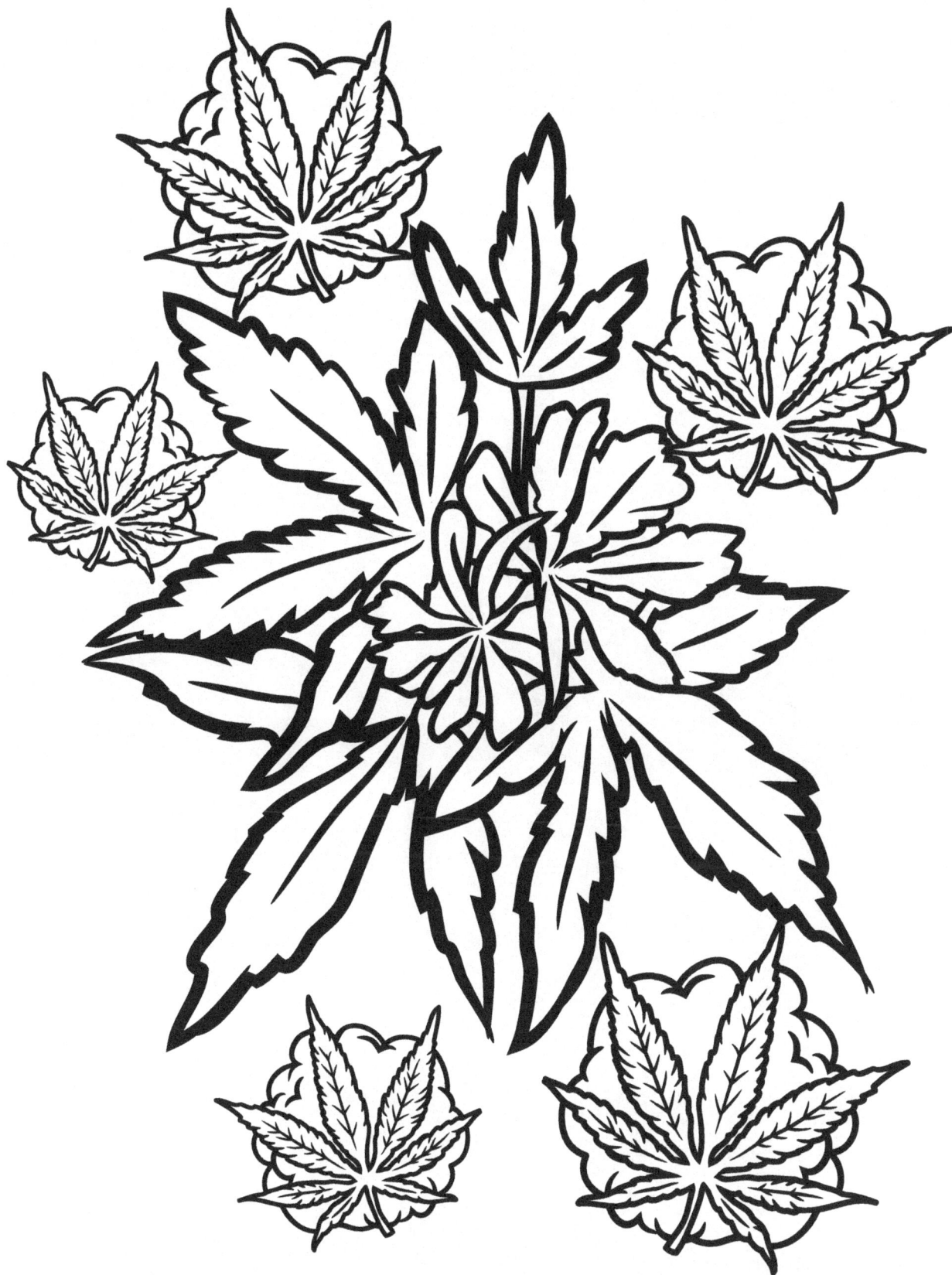

"Forget not that the earth delights to feel your bare feet
and the winds long to play with your hair."
—Khalil Gibran

"A weed is no more than a flower in disguise."
—James Russell Lowell

"Silence is not an absence but a presence."
- Anne D. LeClaire

"You just have to take a deep breath, relax and let the game come to you." -A. J. Green

"True love cannot be found where it does not exist, nor can it be denied where it does."
- Torquato Tasso

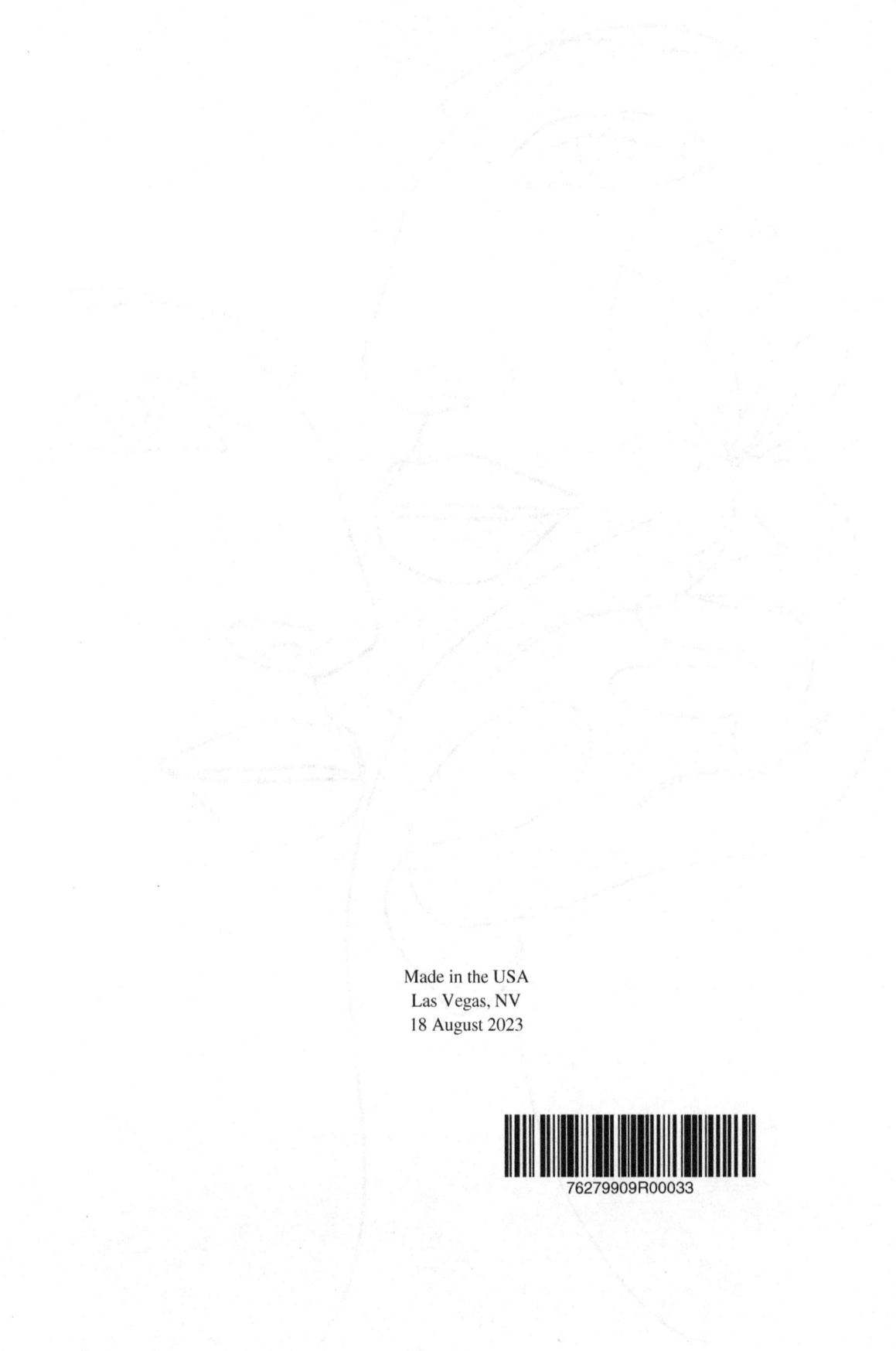

Made in the USA
Las Vegas, NV
18 August 2023